This delightful book is the latest in the series of Ladybird books that have been specially planned to help grown-ups with the world about them.

As in the other books in this series, the large, clear script, the careful choice of words, the frequent repetition and the thoughtful matching of text with pictures all enable grown-ups to think they have taught themselves to cope. The subject of the book will greatly appeal to grown-ups.

Series 999

THE LADYBIRD
BOOKS FOR GROWN-UPS SERIES

MINDFULNESS

by

J. A. HAZELEY, N.S.F.W. and J. P. MORRIS, O.M.G.

(Authors of 'TV's Fiftiest Great Sausage Moments')

Publishers: Ladybird Books Ltd, Loughborough
Printed in England. If wet, Italy.

Mindfulness is the skill of thinking you are doing something when you are doing nothing.

One of the good things about mindfulness is that you get to do a lot of sitting down.

Sitting down is good for the mind because so much positive energy is stored in the lap.

People who practise mindfulness first find somewhere quiet to sit down.

Alan is sitting down in the Falkland Islands.

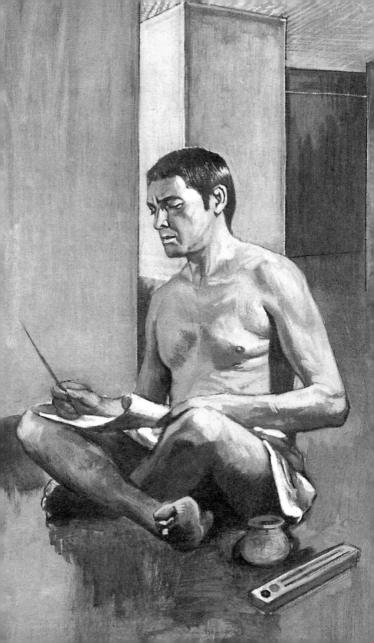

Sophie is concentrating on her breath. It smells of Frazzles.

She says she has light for breakfast, air for lunch and love for supper, but Sophie has also secretly had some Frazzles.

Wendell achieves a state of mindfulness by imagining he is floating in a beautiful lake until his mind empties of everyday worries.

Soon he is aware of himself, but no longer worried about money, work, family or whether he left the taps on.

Many home insurance policies now cover Acts of Mindfulness.

Anna has emptied her mind and is just listening to the world around her.

She can hear the neighbours arguing, two ambulances, a burglar alarm, a child crying, and the sound of dubstep coming from a Subaru Impreza.

She is also concentrating on her own feelings, like her cystitis.

People learn a lot about themselves from mindfulness.

Mindfulness has taught Django to live in the moment.

He used to live in the Peak District.

The sign reads:

ALBION

TO *Winchester,*
ASHUELOT
NASHUA
KEENE and
STATIONS ON THE
FITCHBURG
ROAD

Mindfulness has taught Leanne to accept things as they are: rubbish, expensive, unfair and out-of-date every six months.

It has also taught her to accept things like cake.

Leanne likes cake.

"There is more wisdom in a waterfall than there is in a hundred men," says Jake.

Jake is always saying things like this.

His ex-wife's sister calls him Jerk.

Declan is so mindful that he has forgotten to take his car in for its MoT test.

Alison has been staring at this beautiful tree for five hours.

She was meant to be in the office. Tomorrow she will be fired.

In this way, mindfulness will have solved her work-related stress.

Clive likes to practise loving-kindness meditation. This is where someone thinks of a friend, then sends them love.

Clive finds this easier than bothering to meet his friends or lending them money.

Fleur is on a silent retreat. She likes going on retreat because it takes days and nobody demands anything of her.

Today, a guest speaker is giving a silent speech, after which there will be a silent question-and-answer session.

It is all very different from life in the Leicester parking shop where she works. The clock there is very noisy.

Thaddeus has been practising self-realisation for five years.

He has come to realise his true self, as an air conditioning engineer.

He does not miss being Chancellor of the Exchequer.

Mia has found a spiritual retreat in west London.

This is a shame, as she was hoping her husband would pay for her to go to Thailand.

You can achieve mindfulness anywhere, simply by filling your mind with images of calm, serenity or wonder.

By practising mindfulness, Martin has found inner peace – even though he is being kidnapped by swans.

Valentine became a Buddhist because he was interested in dharma.

Dharma is a word for cosmic law and order.

Valentine is sad. He thought dharma was a type of curry.

In ancient times, Guru Bhellenc entered a state of mindfulness that lasted thirty-five years.

During this time, he thought about everything.

When he had finished, he wrote the answer on a grain of rice.

He never married.

Sometimes life can be too noisy.

Try not speaking for a while.

Let people know what you want with a smile or a frown or by throwing your keys at the back of their head.

Jane has tried many ways of energising and detoxing.

She went on a raw food diet, but the chicken made her very poorly.

Then her tutor told her to "be like water". Jane thought this was a good idea.

Now, just like water, she is drunk most lunchtimes.

Todd likes extreme mindfulness.

Today he is emptying his mind on a tight-rope high above Poole harbour.

The people on the pleasure cruiser below hope that Todd doesn't empty any other part of his body.

New sorts of mindfulness are popping up all the time. This is aqua mindfulness.

There are now courses for cardio mindfulness, cockney mindfulness, honey-roast mindfulness, micro mindfulness and mindlessness.

In mindlessness, you have to beat up your inner total stranger.

Catriona is in love with the earth, but she worries that it does not love her back.

Maybe joining Friends of the Earth was a mistake. Now the earth will never see her as more than that.

Tom and Mozart have gone on a rafting retreat in California.

With only a bottle of water and an inspirational haiku, they must find their way to a state of intense curiosity and awareness.

They are lost and tired, and Mozart wants to give up and go and find some hookers.

Laura tried mindfulness to get in touch with her inner child.

It turns out that Laura's inner child had been prescribed an experimental cough medicine, and was having some very vivid dreams.

Poor Laura.

The authors would like to thank the illustrators whose work they have so
mercilessly ribbed, and whose glorious craftsmanship was the set-dressing of their
childhoods. The inspiration they sparked has never faded.

MICHAEL JOSEPH

UK | USA | Canada | Ireland | Australia
India | New Zealand | South Africa

Michael Joseph is part of the Penguin Random House group of companies
whose addresses can be found at global.penguinrandomhouse.com

Penguin
Random House
UK

First published 2015
003

Copyright © Jason Hazeley and Joel Morris, 2015
All images copyright © Ladybird Books Ltd, 2015

The moral right of the authors has been asserted

Printed in Italy by L.E.G.O. S.p.A

A CIP catalogue record for this book is available from the British Library

ISBN: 978–0–718–18352–3

www.greenpenguin.co.uk

MIX
Paper from
responsible sources
FSC® C018179

Penguin Random House is committed to a
sustainable future for our business, our readers
and our planet. This book is made from Forest
Stewardship Council® certified paper.